W9-CHD-608

Kids
Can
Code

Understanding Coding with

RUBY

Patricia Harris

PowerKiDS press.

New York

Published in 2016 by The Rosen Publishing Group, Inc.
29 East 21st Street, New York, NY 10010

First Edition

Editor: Greg Roza
Book Design: Michael J. Flynn

Photo Credits: Cover Margot Petrowski/Shutterstock.com; cover, pp. 1, 3–24 (coding background) Lukas Rs/Shutterstock.com; p. 5 Robert Daly/Caiaimage/Getty Images; p. 6 Darrin Henry/Shutterstock.com; pp. 9, 15 Monkey Business Images/Shutterstock.com; pp. 11, 19 racorn/Shutterstock.com; pp. 12–13 (Ruby screenshots) courtesy of www.ruby-lang.org; p. 13 (boy) Shyamalamuralinath/Shutterstock.com; p. 21 Thomas Barwick/Iconica/Getty Images.

Library of Congress Cataloging-in-Publication Data

Harris, Patricia.
Understanding coding with Ruby / by Patricia Harris.
p. cm. — (Kids can code)
Includes index.
ISBN 978-1-5081-4450-2 (pbk.)
ISBN 978-1-5081-4451-9 (6-pack)
ISBN 978-1-5081-4452-6 (library binding)
1. Computer programming — Juvenile literature. 2. Coding theory — Juvenile literature. I. Harris, Patricia, 1949-. II. Title.
QA76.64 H37 2016
005.133—d23

Manufactured in the United States of America

CPSIA Compliance Information: Batch #BW16PK: For Further Information contact Rosen Publishing, New York, New York at 1-800-237-9932

Contents

Introduction to Ruby..................4

Images vs. Text......................6

Planning Stage 8

Print and Put.......................10

Exploring the Environment...........12

Hello World! 14

User Input..........................16

Stick to the Plan...................18

Ruby Rocks!.........................20

Glossary............................23

Index...............................24

Websites............................24

Introduction to Ruby

In 1843, programing pioneer Ada Lovelace wrote the first computer program. Since then, many coders have followed in her footsteps. Today, we have dozens of **computer languages** available for use in programming, and each one has its strengths and weaknesses. Ruby programming language is easy to use and has lots of possibilities. This makes it the perfect program to start coding with.

Ruby is a traditional written-code language. It uses words and symbols rather than pictures to help users code. Ruby is also called an object-oriented program. This means that it's based on the use of "objects" rather than actions. Objects can be organized into classes, which allows them to be grouped together for easier coding.

Breaking the Code

Ruby is open-source **software**. That means anyone can use it, modify it, and distribute it. Users need to **download** Ruby or find it on their computer before they can use it.

You might think coding is only for experts and scientists, but it's not. You can start coding with Ruby and the other programs in this series right away.

Images vs. Text

Some coding languages use drag-and-drop images instead of text. The programs Scratch and Hopscotch use a graphical user interface, or GUI (GOO-ee), to allow users to communicate with the computer. Unlike these two image-based programming languages, Ruby is a traditional written-code language. It uses lines of text and symbols to give a computer instructions to be **executed** in Ruby. Because of this, Ruby users need to know a set of special words called **commands**. These words tell the program how to respond, or they tell users important information.

Even though Scratch and Hopscotch are easier to use, Ruby is more powerful and offers users more options. It's also a step closer to using more difficult written-code languages, such as C++, Perl, and Java.

Commands are key to getting Ruby to do what you want it to. These are some of the most common Ruby commands. Refer back to this list as you continue reading about Ruby.

SOME COMMON COMMANDS IN RUBY

chomp – Tells Ruby to ignore line breaks, and makes sure responses are displayed on a single line.

comment – Text in Ruby code that is meant to guide the coder and is not part of the program. Use the # symbol to start a single-line comment. Use =begin and =end to add a multiple-line comment.

elsif – Used when user **input** could result in multiple answers, such as "What is your favorite color?"

gets – Tells Ruby to collect user input, such as the user's name.

if/else – Allows Ruby to make a decision based on input.

nil – An object without value. It's also Ruby's way of saying "I'm done."

print/puts – Displays the results of a program on the screen.

Planning Stage

Before you can begin to learn about coding in any language, Ruby included, you need to know that computer programming is about following rules. Yes, that sounds a lot like playing a game, and it can be just as much fun.

Rule 1: Coders must know what they want the computer to do and write a plan.

Rule 2: Coders must use special words to have the computer take input, make choices, and take action.

Rule 3: Coders need to think about what tasks can be put into a group.

Rule 4: Coders need to use **logic** with AND, OR, NOT, and other **logic** statements as key words.

Rule 5: Coders must explore the **environment** and understand how it works.

Breaking the Code

Ruby is written in a text editor and run in a **terminal** window on your computer. That means you have a two-step process. Because Ruby is an easy language to use, you'll find this process easy once you see how it works.

9

Ruby is a programming language that uses English words and several special characters with special meanings. Sometimes the English words mean just what you expect, but sometimes they have different meanings.

The command "print" displays the results of the code you typed. If you write the command "print 5," the computer displays "5=> nil" on your screen. The command "print 4 + 5" displays "9=> nil." The math work is built in.

Another command that looks like English is "puts." It also displays what you tell it on the screen, but using more than one line. So if you say "puts 4 + 5," your screen shows the output on two lines instead of one, like this:

```
9
= > nil
```

"Nil" is an object like all the other objects in Ruby. It's an object without a value. "Nil" is also Ruby's way of saying "I'm done, and I've got nothing to add."

Breaking the Code

Unlike in English writing, the period is not used at the end of sentences or commands. It's used in special cases to add a special command. More on that later.

Exploring the Environment

Before you can begin to work, you must understand the environment in which Ruby works. To write your program, you need a program called a text editor. Most computers come with a text editor installed, but there are many others you can download. The text editor allows you to write code, but it doesn't show the results. When you are ready to save the document, name the file and change the **extension** to .rb so Ruby will know it's a Ruby file.

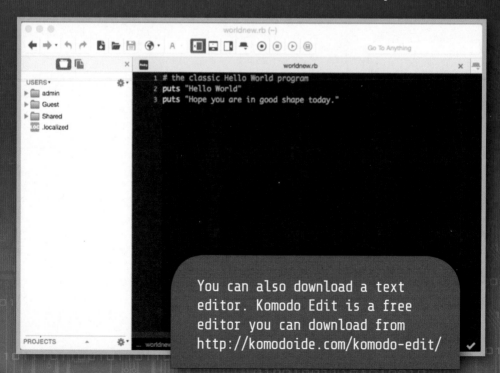

worldnew.rb (~)

Go To Anything

worldnew.rb

USERS▼
▶ admin
▶ Guest
▶ Shared
.localized

```
1 # the classic Hello World program
2 puts "Hello World"
3 puts "Hope you are in good shape today."
```

PROJECTS

worldnew

You can also download a text editor. Komodo Edit is a free editor you can download from http://komodoide.com/komodo-edit/

After your program is written and saved, open Ruby on your computer to see it. On Apple computers, you need to open a terminal window and type in "irb" to open Ruby. On PCs, the Ruby program appears under the Start Menu.

```
● ● ●                            ⌂              — bash — 80×24
Last login: Mon Jun 15 15:21:57 on ttys000
PD-iMac:~ guest$ ruby worldnew.rb
```

This is the terminal screen on an Apple Computer. You can use it to display the results of the code you wrote in the text editor.

Hello World!

The first program many beginning coders write when using a traditional written-code language such as Ruby is the Hello World program. You must have a plan for every program. The plan is to tell the computer to display the words "Hello World." This is a very simple plan, and the code is also very simple.

```
1   # a simple program to print out Hello World
2   puts "Hello World"
```

Notice line 1 starts with #. Use that symbol when adding a comment to your code. For a longer program, you can use several lines to type out the plan. Here is the code with a longer comment:

```
1   =begin
2   a simple program to print out Hello World
3   this is often the first program written
4   =end
5   puts "Hello World"
```

You can make this program print more lines just by adding to the program.

```
1  =begin
2  Adding more text to the program to print out Hello World
3  it is still just printing out what you tell it to
4  =end
5  puts "Hello World"
6  puts "I am glad to see everyone today."
7  puts "Goodbye!"
```

You can have fun writing this simple code and running it in the terminal. Remember to always use the file extension .rb, so the file name looks like this: filename.rb.

User Input

Here's the plan for a program that requires user input: Ask the user to enter his or her name and then print a message with the name included. If you don't know what all these commands do, turn to the chart on page 7.

```
1   =begin
2   This is a program to ask the user's name and display it.
3   Make sure the name starts with a capital letter even if the
4   user does not put one in.
5   =end
6   puts "Hello Computer User"
7   puts "Please tell me your name."
8   name = gets.chomp
9   puts "#{name}, I hope you are having fun today."
```

You can add new commands to a program that's already written and make coding quicker. The new code in line 9 below makes sure the name is capitalized.

```
8    name = gets.chomp
9    name.capitalize!
10   puts "#{name}, I hope you are having fun today."
```

The dot before "capitalize" is an example of a method in Ruby. Methods are sets of premade instructions—in this case, capitalizing the first letter of a word. An exclamation point in Ruby means a permanent change is taking place.

You can use logic to make your program more interesting. The commands "if" and "else" allow the program to make a choice based on the input. "If" the answer is "yes," the program answers "Great!" "If" the answer is anything "else," the program gives a different answer.

```ruby
10  puts "#{name}, I hope you are having fun today."
11  #Now we are asking for an answer
12  puts "Tell me yes or no."
13  answer = gets.chomp
14  #the next line makes the answer all lowercase
15  #no matter how it was entered
16  answer.downcase!
17  #Here is the If…ELSE part
18  if answer == "yes"
19    puts "Great!"
20  else
21    puts "You need to do more Ruby work."
22  end
23
```

Stick to the Plan

Now that you know how easy it is to code with Ruby, it's your turn to make a program. As with all programs, you first need to come up with a plan and stick to it as you code.

PLAN

Ask the user's name and ask if their favorite color is red, blue, green, yellow, or pink. Then display responses based on the answer.

You will need to use a new command: elsif. Notice that the spelling is tricky! This useful command lets you have more than one "else" answer. As with the if/else commands, start the code with an "if" command. Since there's more than one possible answer, use the "elsif" command for each color instead of the "else" command. The answer for this program is on page 22.

Coders often work together on a project. You can share your code with a friend through email.

What is your name?

What is your favorite color?
red, blue, green, yellow, or pink

19

Ruby Rocks!

By now, you can probably see that coding isn't just for scientists, computer experts, and geniuses. Anyone can code—especially with a program like Ruby! Once you have a plan and understand some special commands, you can start coding.

Here's a helpful list of steps to get you coding with Ruby in no time!

1. Write a simple plan. Think about how parts can be grouped.
2. Open your text editor.
3. Write a comment to tell what the program will do.
4. Save your work with the extension .rb. Be sure your editor put the program in your home directory.
5. Start writing code to fit your plan.
6. Add comments in your program whenever you're going to do a new action. Comments will help you remember what's happening.
7. Save your program as you go along and when you think you're finished.
8. On an Apple computer, open the terminal window. At the prompt, type in "ruby yourfilename.rb"
9. On a PC, go to Open Ruby in the Start menu, then open yourfilename.rb
10. Run your program with a friend and enjoy!

You can start coding with Ruby right now! Once you've done that, you can move on to other programming languages.

```
1   =begin
2     This is a program to ask the user's name and use it.
3     The program will also use an IF...ELSIF statement
4     to find out which of five choices is the favorite color choice.
5     It will make an appropriate response.
6   =end
7   puts "Hello Computer User."
8   puts "Please tell me your name."
9   name = gets.chomp
10  #.chomp is used to take out an unwanted line when the name
11  #is used in the middle of a sentence
12  name.capitalize!
13  #remember capitalize! makes the first letter capital
14  puts "#{name}, I want to know which color you like best of the ones I list."
15  #Now we are asking for an answer
16  puts "Choose one of the following colors:"
17  puts "red, blue, green, yellow, or pink."
18  answer = gets.chomp
19  #the next line makes the answer all lowercase
20  #no matter how it was entered
21  answer.downcase!
22  # using elsif for choices
23  if "red" == answer
24    puts "AH HA! Your choice is red."
25  elsif "blue" == answer
26    puts "AH HA! Your choice is blue."
27  elsif "green" == answer
28    puts "AH HA! Your choice is green."
29  elsif "yellow" == answer
30    puts "AH HA! Your choice is yellow."
31  elsif "pink" == answer
32    puts "AH HA! Your choice is pink."
33  else
34    puts "AH HA! Your choice is not in my list."
35  end
```

Glossary

command: A code or message that tells a computer to do something.

computer language: A programming language designed to give instructions to a computer.

download: Copy data from one computer to another, often over the Internet.

environment: The combination of computer hardware and software that allows a user to perform various tasks.

execute: To carry out or put into effect, such as a plan.

extension: The letters at the end of a file name that tells what kind of program will open it.

input: Information that is entered into a computer.

logic: A proper or reasonable way of thinking about or understanding something.

software: A program that runs on a computer and performs certain tasks.

terminal: A computer screen or window where computer data can be viewed.

Index

A

characters, 10
chomp, 7
commands, 6, 7, 10,
    16, 17, 18, 20
comment, 7, 14, 20
computer languages, 4,
    6, 9, 10, 21

E

elsif, 7, 18
environment, 8, 12
extension, 12, 15, 20

G

gets, 7
GUI, 6

H

Hello World program,
    14

I

if/else, 7, 17, 18
input, 7, 8, 16, 17

L

logic, 8, 17
Lovelace, Ada, 4

M

methods, 16

N

nil, 7, 10

O

object-oriented
    program, 4
objects, 4, 7, 10

P

plan, 8, 14, 16, 18, 19,
    20
print/put, 7, 10, 16
program, 4, 6, 7, 12,
    13, 14, 15, 16, 17,
    18, 20, 22
programming, 4, 8

R

rules, 8

T

text editor, 9, 12, 13, 20

U

user, 16

W

written-code language,
    4, 6, 10, 14

Websites

Due to the changing nature of Internet links, PowerKids Press has developed an online list of websites related to the subject of this book. This site is updated regularly. Please use this link to access the list: www.powerkidslinks.com/kcc/ruby